# LOST NEWPORT

# Lost Newport

## Vanished Cottages
## of the Resort Era

### REVISED EDITION

*Paul F. Miller*

APPLEWOOD BOOKS
Carlisle, Massachusetts

Published in cooperation with
The Preservation Society of Newport County

An abbreviated version of this survey appeared in
*Newport History: Journal of the Newport Historical Society*
in Fall 2005 and Spring 2006.

ISBN 978-1-4290-9112-1

Thank you for purchasing an Applewood book.
Applewood reprints America's lively classics —
books from the past that are still of interest to
modern readers. For a free copy of our current
catalog, please write to Applewood Books,
P. O. Box 27, Carlisle, MA 01741.

www.awb.com

*Book design by Barbara DaSilva*

Manufactured in the U.S.A.

# TABLE OF CONTENTS

*Introduction*
Page 7

*Cottages of the North End*
Page 13

*Cottages of Central Newport*
Page 25

*Cottages of Bellevue Avenue*
Page 51

*Cottages of Ocean Avenue*
Page 107

*Notes*
Page 133

*Credits*
Page 135

*Index to the Cottages*
Page 139

*To Charles J. Burns*
*for his continuous and unerring encouragement*

# Acknowledgments

This book is adapted from *Lost Houses of Newport*, an exhibit on display from 11 June to 31 October 2005 at The Elms, a property operated by the Preservation Society of Newport County, on the occasion of the Society's sixtieth anniversary. A debt of gratitude is owed to those who have previously, in varying fashions, addressed this subject: Claus von Bulow and Tom Hagerman in a 1975 photo exhibition for the Preservation Society, Newport historian Francis X. Girr in his scholarly research, photographer John T. Hopf in his insightful *Newport—Then and Now* (1989), and Leonard J. Panaggio in his evocative *Grist Mill* column for the *Newport Daily News*. The author also extends thanks to Historic New England; the *Newport Daily News*; the Newport Historical Society; the Redwood Library and Athenaeum; Shepley, Bulfinch, Richardson and Abbott; and Gustave J.S. White, Inc.

The following individuals provided invaluable assistance: Ms. Patricia M. Anton, Ms. Theodora Aspegren, Mr. Charles J. Burns, Ms. Alice Campbell, Mr. David Chase, Mr. Michael R. Corcoran, Mr. Walton Craig, Ms. Severine Fleming, Mr. Robert Kelly, Mr. Bertram Lippincott, Ms. Stacey Lyon, Ms. Laura M. Murphy, Mr. Brian W. O'Reilly, Mrs. Eugene J. O'Reilly, Mrs. Monique Panaggio, Mr. Benjamin C. Reed, Mr. Lloyd Michael Rivers, Mrs. Diana Lanier Smith, Ms. Claudia E. Thiel, Mrs. Harle Tinney, Mr. James L.Yarnall, Mr. Thomas E. Zinn, and above all Mr. John G. Winslow.

The majority of the images are drawn from the archives of The Preservation Society of Newport County, 424 Bellevue Avenue, Newport, RI 02840 unless otherwise cited.

# Introduction

*V*eteran world travelers visiting Newport, Rhode Island, in the first years of the twentieth century were as impressed as neophytes by the sheer concentration of opulent summer villas ringing this old colonial seaport. Grand Duke Boris of Russia's paean to the resort struck a characteristic chord: "I have never dreamed of such luxury as I have seen at Newport." Yet in the ranks of *habitués* of the cottage colony stood a few more candid and prescient critics. Henry James in commenting on the disappearance of the *pure* spirit of the Newport of his youth lamented that "the white elephants, as one may best call them, all cry and no wool, all house and no garden, make now, for three or four miles, a barely interrupted chain...while their inverted owners, roused from a witless dream, wonder what in the world is to be done with them."

Within a few decades, James's observation would prove prophetic. Two world wars, a long depression, the introduction of a permanent income tax, high inheritance and real estate taxes, and the shortage of available domestic staff made Newport summer cottages, gradually and almost imperceptibly, anachronisms. With the evaporation of the market for large seasonal homes, the primary hope for the survival of these former cottages seemed in conversion to schools, as hauntingly evoked by Grace Kelly's Newport socialite character Tracy Lord in the 1956 Warner Bros. film *High Society*. And so, by the 1950s, much of the central Bellevue Avenue estate corridor was thus converted; nursing homes and apartment houses joined the ranks but educational institutions dominated, the chief landowners becoming Vernon Court Junior College, Salve Regina University, La Salle Academy, St. Catherine's Academy, and Hatch Preparatory School. As not all summer houses could be saved, difficult choices had to be made, and were it not for these institutions much of Bellevue Avenue would have been cleared for new development and subdivision. This response was the only then rational move to counter the loss of city tax revenues formerly generated by summer estates. Simultaneously, however, the city's economy moved away from dependency on the summer colony to hosting a major U.S. naval station with related defense industries. This, together with the development opportunities fostered by the completion of the Newport Bridge in 1969, ushered in an era of prosperous suburbanization.

Newport Daily News,
*March 19, 1973*

Post–World War II prosperity also brought with it a desire for swift change which, when faced with "redundant" architecture, proved merciless. The colonial wharves of Newport disappeared primarily in the 1960s due to urban renewal and the creation of a new central arterial road designed to render downtown Newport more accessible. In the process, however, local historic preservation movements reacted strongly and gained unprecedented impetus. Reaction had begun when Mrs. Katherine U. Warren and friends founded The Preservation Society of Newport County in 1945, initially to save the 1749 Hunter House from demolition for the extension of naval facilities. In 1968 Miss Doris Duke joined her with the creation of the Newport Restoration Foundation, which purchased and restored close to ninety primarily Colonial-era homes.

The success of such private preservation efforts is today so apparent that it is often taken for granted. To the first-time or casual visitor to Newport, a drive down the former main artery of the summer colony that is Bellevue Avenue still impresses with its seemingly uninterrupted alignment of exemplary nineteenth- and early-twentieth-century domestic architecture. On closer glimpse, or on foot, however, it becomes readily apparent that there are holes in the fabric. Virtually every block, and more so on the subsidiary cross streets, has lost a cottage of some local or frequently national merit. The majority of these homes were demolished for residential or commercial subdivision rather than by natural causes such as fire. Luckily, the very density of the cottage colony, with such an architectural *embarras de richesses,* masks such intrusions.

*Ocean House Hotel [1846], Russell Warren, architect*

This contextual density of cottage architecture is one of the unique facets of Newport. Unlike the model of a country house, the social and physical amenities of a rural landed seat did not apply here. The summer residents of Newport began by building freestanding, timber-framed cottages in the early nineteenth century, on what were essentially suburban-size lots ringing the existing colonial town. Minimally landscaped, these lots provided views across open meadows to the harbor or sea. The colony's social life was, at first, simple and literary: social life focused on the reception rooms of a handful of boarding houses or hotels and a series of private clubs. As social and architectural ambitions grew, particularly after the Civil War, with an explosion of new fortunes in finance, industry, mining, and transit, the lot size rarely did. This led to the curious sight of progressively larger Beaux Arts–style villas being erected on the site of earlier Gothic, Greek revival, or Italianate cottages, with scant breathing room.

The scope of this survey is related to cottages built in the golden age of Newport's reign as the queen of resorts, roughly from 1830 to 1930. We will not consider, at this time, the many cottages demolished during the Gilded Age to make way for larger, perhaps more architecturally significant houses on their sites. A large enough number of these houses survive today to give us an impression of their charm but impress more often for their predictable, often formulaic, construction. This is not to appear arbitrary nor to dismiss them altogether, for each, no doubt, was significant in its day and had important historical associations; witness the summer home of George Bancroft, historian and statesman, which hosted Bancroft's horticultural experiments to perfect the 'American Beauty' rose and meetings of the nation's literati, but which was leveled to make way for McKim, Mead & White's extraordinary Rosecliff of 1902.

Emphasis is given instead to those vanished cottages whose sites were either developed for structures not in sympathy with the earlier use of the lot or which were not replaced at all. Nor do we wish this survey to be viewed as comprehensive, for at present photographic evidence is lacking for at least a dozen interesting vanished homes. It is hoped that with time such views will surface and also that any errors or omissions in the text will be corrected through future research. We enthusiastically welcome such revision.

Top: *Bancroft Cottage,*
*demolished for Rosecliff*
Bottom: *Merritt Cottage,*
*demolished for The Elms*

*Oakland Farm, ca. 1906, Portsmouth, RI*
*[demolished], country estate of*
*Cornelius II and Alfred G. Vanderbilt*

It should also be pointed out that country estates, with farms, gardens, manor house and dependencies, stable and riding rings, and similar such amenities, did exist outside Newport, scattered across Aquidneck Island, with many dating back to the eighteenth century. Although acquired by such leading summer colonist families as the Vanderbilts as a casual corollary to and closely interrelated with Newport social life, any listing of the farms would detract from the scope of a study of the cottage colony. Today these farms are a largely lost legacy.

*Oakland Farm riding ring, ca. 1906*
*[demolished]*

Although the following cottage inventory may seem to range stylistically from the ordinary to the sublime, it is the cumulative absence of these selected cottages from the grandeur of the ensemble that we aim to evoke. The ensemble seemed to teeter in the balance until the 1962 purchase by a group of friends, on behalf of the Preservation Society, of The Elms. This estate block, comprising the 1901 Beaux Arts–style E.J. Berwind villa by architect Horace Trumbauer and a sizable formal garden, had been sold at public auction and was awaiting demolition. It constituted a major leap of faith for Mrs. Warren to intervene in saving a large early-twentieth-century cottage, knowing that its future would be dependent on funds generated by public visitation. Although the Society had been seasonally opening, under its auspices, Cornelius Vanderbilt II's The Breakers since 1947, the purchase of the Berwind property seemed to many to be tempting fate. The favorable public response amazed all who had heretofore felt that the Society should remain a guardian of colonial Newport. In the following decade eight more properties were acquired, through purchase and gift, all of them nineteenth-century summer homes in a range of styles; together they provide a comprehensive, contextual guide to the evolution of American domestic architecture, from the colonial to the Beaux Arts. Strengthened further through adaptive reuse fostered by the condominium market, active in Newport since 1973, and historic district ordinances introduced in 1965, the future of the cottage colony seems optimistic. Although it is logical to assume that additional great Newport cottages will someday fall victim to natural disaster or to economic downturns, it is hoped that knowing what previously stood on key sites and what contributed to making Newport a unique American architectural microcosm might remind inhabitants and visitors of the fragility of the surviving balance and perhaps inspire them to be sensitive to past architectural traditions in future construction.

Paul F. Miller, Curator

MAP
OF
THE CITY OF
NEWPORT
RHODE ISLAND
WITH PRINCIPAL POINTS OF INTEREST
AND SUMMER RESIDENCES WITH NAMES OF OWNERS

1937

# Cottages of the North End

*F.W. Andrews House by H.H. Richardson, ca. 1895*

# FRANK W. ANDREWS HOUSE *(1873)*
## SUNSET LAWN
*Henry Hobson Richardson, architect*
*Maple Avenue*
*Demolished*

Engulfed by the 1940s expansion of the U.S. Naval Station, the Maple Avenue estate district was known in the early twentieth century for its sweeping views of Narragansett Bay and surrounding countryside dotted with restored Revolutionary War earthworks. Richardson, assisted by Charles Follen McKim as draftsman, planned a cavernous Queen Anne–style summer home for the Andrews family of Boston, to embrace these views. For the house's exterior, the architect experimented with combinations of patterned shingles and clapboards. The Andrews villa's ground floor interior space centered around a living hall and comprised 6,000 square feet, then the largest floor plan of any Newport cottage. This structure became an important design source for the development of H.H. Richardson's Queen Anne style in such succeeding projects as the 1874–76 William Watts Sherman House in Newport. Badly damaged by fire, the Andrews house was subsequently torn down and is now the site of a residential subdivision.

*Castlewood, garden facade, ca. 1920*

*Castlewood, "Louis XVI" drawing room, ca. 1910*

*Castlewood, entrance facade, ca. 1906*

## HOUSE Nº· 2

### CASTLEWOOD *(1905)*
*Mrs. Emile Bruguiere Estate*
*Edward Payson Whitman, architect*
*Maple Avenue and Girard Avenue*
*Demolished*

Dominating the highest point of land at Coddington Point, this white-trimmed brick neoclassical-style villa was visible from all of southern Narragansett Bay. Josephine Bruguiere of California, daughter of San Francisco banker Pedar Sather, founder of the Sather Banking Co., incorporated the remnants of an eighteenth-century battery thought to have been erected by the Comte de Rochambeau into the formal gardens. The interior featured high-style French reception rooms in Renaissance and Louis XV taste. Josephine Bruguiere, remembered for her lavish entertaining, filed bankruptcy in August of 1914. Returning from Europe she was drowned in the sinking of the White Star liner *Arabic*, torpedoed August 19, 1915. Castlewood was sold to Arnold Watson Essex and then by his estate in 1916 to Mr. John H. Hanan of New York, a millionaire shoe manufacturer. Following Hanan's death in 1920 Castlewood was converted into an orphanage, the Mercy Home and School, and demolished by the U.S. government for World War II public housing for workers of the Newport torpedo and naval ordnance factories. A Louis XV–style paneled room was removed by Mrs. Bruguiere and has been incorporated into a contemporary French house on Ocean Avenue.

*Castlewood,
entrance hall
(left),
dining room
(center),
and salon
(bottom),
1906*

*Philbrick Cottage, 1876*

## HOUSE Nº·3

## EDWARD S. PHILBRICK COTTAGE *(1874)*
*Coddington Point*
*S.J. Brown, architect*
*Demolished*

During the 1870s, Coddington Point, a somewhat retired but desirable waterfront locale, witnessed the construction of a series of picturesque villas along a new shore road called Coddington Avenue. Chief among them was the 1874 Philbrick House, a gable-roofed "stick style" timber-framed cottage built by the Boston architect S.J. Brown for the Philbrick family of Boston. Sold in December 1899 to Theresa D. Weld (Mrs. A. Winsor Weld) of Newton, Massachusetts, the property was, together with the nearby villas of Kate Hunter Dunn (G.C. Mason, architect, 1878); Hugh L. Willoughby; and C. Francis Bates, requisitioned by the city of Newport for expansion of the Newport Naval Station. Sold in August 1918 to the city of Newport for $1 dollar, the cottage was demolished and the site transferred to the United States government for naval purposes.

## JOHN BANNISTER HOUSE *(CA. 1756)*
### *West Main Road*
### *(located just past the Newport-Middletown city line)*
### *Demolished*

This distinguished mid eighteenth-century rusticated Georgian country house was built for colonial architect Peter Harrison's brother-in-law and was renovated by Harrison. The house was demolished between 1953 and 1955 for an elementary school. Salvaged interiors and the main staircase were purchased by Henry Francis du Pont for his Winterthur Museum.

Left:*Bannister House, 1947*

*Dudley Place, ca. 1920*

## CHARLES DUDLEY HOUSE (CA. 1750)
*Attributed to Peter Harrison, architect*
*West Main Road at Miantonomi Avenue*
*(city line at One Mile Corner)*
*Demolished*

Built as a country retreat for Royal Customs Collector Charles Dudley, this square three-story house of wood painted and sanded to resemble stone was one of colonial Newport's most architecturally distinguished domestic structures. The upper two stories were treated in the manner of a neoclassical rusticated pavilion decorated with Ionic pilasters rising to a low-hipped roof. Long associated with the Bull family of Newport, the house was baptized Dudley Place and converted to a summer residence in the nineteenth century. In 1882–83 McKim, Mead, & White, architects, renovated the historic house for Charles M. Bull. The property saw a further renaissance when purchased in 1927 by William K. Vanderbilt Jr. for his daughter Muriel Fair Vanderbilt, then Mrs. Frederic Cameron Church Jr. and subsequently Mrs. Henry D. Phelps. A riding ring and stable were added to the rear of the estate for Mrs. Phelps, a lifelong equestrienne. Following divorce from Mr. Phelps in 1936, Dudley Place was closed when Muriel Vanderbilt moved to California. Upon her return following World War II, the vicinity had become commercialized by the expansion of the nearby U.S. Naval Base and the property was left abandoned until sold for demolition in 1953; a gas station, a motel, and several residential subdivisions now occupy the site, although the stable block was spared and has been rehabilitated for condominium residences.

MAP — OF
NEWPORT
THE CITY OF
RHODE ISLAND
WITH PRINCIPAL POINTS OF INTEREST
AND SUMMER RESIDENCES WITH NAMES OF OWNERS

1937

# Cottages of
# Central Newport

*Whitehall, ca. 1900*

*Whitehall, in a derelict state, ca. 1930*

*Whitehall, ca. 1897*

HOUSE N⁰· 6

## WHITEHALL *(1894)*
*David H. King Jr. Estate*
*McKim, Mead & White, architects*
*Catherine Street and Rhode Island Avenue*
*Demolished*

Whitehall was built by McKim, Mead & White, in their newly popular Colonial revival style for a favorite client, New York building contractor and developer David H. King. In 1903, the estate was purchased by New York real estate baron John Jay Coogan and used in season by his family until seriously damaged by fire on March 10, 1911. Due to the simultaneous remodeling of the family's Fifth Avenue residence, restoration work in Newport was postponed. With the 1915 death of Mr. Coogan, the house remained unoccupied. Although the family remained sentimentally attached to the estate, major repairs never advanced, and this led to the pervasive legend that the Coogans had been snubbed socially, having issued invitations for a dinner party to which no one came. In point of fact, the popular Harriet G. Coogan was a great-granddaughter of John Lyon Gardiner and inherited from his estate a very large section of the upper end of Manhattan. The property was sold by Mrs. Coogan's son Jay on January 8, 1953, for $23,000 to Albert K. Sherman of Newport, who demolished the house that year for a residential subdivision.

HOUSE N⁰· 7

THE CORNERS *(1872)*
*Miss Charlotte Cushman House*
*Richard Morris Hunt, architect*
*49 Catherine Street*
*Demolished*

Built by Hunt for a close friend, the actress Charlotte Cushman, The
Corners was perhaps the most ambitious of the architect's picturesque
"Swiss chalets" along the Catherine Street corridor. With its dra-
matically corbeled attic balcony, asymmetrical entrance tower, boldly
articulated "stick style" trim, and outswept veranda, the Cushman villa
dominated the intersection of Rhode Island Avenue in the then fashion-
able heart of the cottage colony. Sold by Miss Cushman's estate in 1890
to James H. and Ella L.B. Darlington, the property remained intact until
subsequent sale to Bernice H. (Mrs. Mason D.) Rector in 1938. Severely
damaged shortly thereafter by a fire, the house was demolished and contemporary homes built on the site in the 1950s.

Left: *The Corners, ca. 1935*

## THOMAS G. APPLETON HOUSE *(1871)*

*Richard Morris Hunt, architect*
*Catherine Street*
*Demolished*

Thomas G. Appleton of Boston, a childhood friend of Hunt's, commissioned this highly original and picturesque summer house in the immediate vicinity of Richard and Catherine Hunt's own cottage. The most fully developed of Hunt's "chalets," the Appleton House was known for its projecting balconies; variously shaped dormers; painted shingle roof; and a profusion of posts, brackets, and diagonal braces. The second story included wood shingles and colored slate laid in patterns reminiscent of contemporary French villa architecture. The cottage was sold by Appleton's estate on July 30, 1887, to Emma E. Barret and was subsequently heavily damaged by fire and demolished. The site was incorporated into the grounds of the adjoining Ayrault House and later subdivided.

Left: *T.G. Appleton House, ca. 1875*

Caldwell House, entrance hall as redecorated by J.D. Johnston, ca. 1890

## HOUSE N⁰· 9

## CALDWELL HOUSE *(CA. 1855)*
*Misses Caldwell Estate*
*Kay and Ayrault Streets*
*Demolished*

Built as the summer residence of Boston merchant Caleb Chace, this Italianate summer cottage was acquired by William Shakespeare Caldwell of New York in 1866. In 1890, his daughters commissioned a private chapel and a music room, both with windows by John La Farge, as part of alterations undertaken by the Newport architect J.D. Johnston. Sold on April 20, 1931, to Waldemar Conrad von Zedtwitz, the house was promptly demolished for a residential subdivision. The chapel's stained glass was purchased by the Diocese of Fall River and incorporated into St. Patrick's Convent in that city. In 2004, Salve Regina University acquired the glass from the diocese and returned the windows to Newport for installation in a new campus chapel by Robert A. M. Stern (2010).

# WILLIAM GAMMELL COTTAGE *(CA. 1872)*
*Gammell Estate*
*The Cliffs*
*Demolished*

Built for William Gammell, a distinguished professor at Brown University in Providence, this large Italianate cottage with fanciful bracketed eaves was sold by his estate in 1947 to George Tyson, who had the house demolished for a new one built on the site the following year. Known as North Cottage in the Gammell family, the William Gammell House flanked that of Mrs. Thomas Shaw-Safe (née Harriet Ives Gammell), called Ocean Lawn (extant, 1889), by Peabody & Stearns architects; and that of Mr. R.S. Gammell. The latter Gammell cottage, South Cottage, or Southerly, similar in scale and style to North Cottage, was also to be demolished, in 1955, and its site incorporated into the former Shaw-Safe property by Mr. and Mrs. Harvey S. Firestone.

Left: *Gammell Cottage, ca. 1910*

*H.A.C. Taylor House, entrance facade, 1887*

*H.A.C. Taylor House, garden facade, ca. 1910*

# H.A.C. TAYLOR HOUSE *(1886)*
### *Taylor Estate*
### *McKim, Mead & White, architects*
### *Annandale Road*
### *Demolished*

An icon of Colonial revival architecture in America, McKim, Mead & White's internationally celebrated cottage for Henry Augustus Coit Taylor of New York initiated the Adamseque "colonial" design that continued through the Second World War and, in an abridged fashion, survives in America to the present. The house remained in the family until its sale by Francis Taylor on October 15, 1952, to Barbara L. Holmsen. That year the cottage was demolished for subdivision of its grounds. Some architectural salvage was incorporated into the adjacent outbuildings of Ocean Lawn and into a Colonial revival subdivision, Johnson Terrace, then under construction on East Main Road in Middletown.

*H.A.C. Taylor House, ca. 1947*

*H.A.C. Taylor House, portico, ca. 1947*

*Cliffs, ca. 1875*

## HOUSE N<sup>o.</sup> 12

### THE FEARING COTTAGE [CLIFFS] *(1859)*
*Daniel Fearing House*
*George Champlin Mason, architect (?)*
*Narragansett Avenue at Annandale Road*
*Demolished*

This large Italianate house was built by Daniel Fearing of New York, a noted art collector. The cottage then passed to his grandson Daniel B. Fearing, book collector and mayor of Newport. The house then passed from Mr. Fearing's estate to his nephew, H. A. C. Taylor, and his nephew's wife, Charlotte, to be consolidated within their neighboring property. Taylor's heirs demolished the house following World War II to reduce tax valuations.

*Croquet party, ca. 1865*

*Sheldon Cottage, ca. 1875*

## HOUSE Nº. 13

### FREDERICK SHELDON HOUSE *(CA. 1860)*
*George Champlin Mason, architect*
*Annandale Road*
*Demolished*

With its broad veranda, low-hipped mansard roof, and projecting rear
service ell, this Italianate cottage for Frederick Sheldon of New York was
typical of local architect George Champlin Mason's summer cottages.
A virtual development by him arose in the 1860s for the extended
Fearing-Sheldon-Taylor family in the vicinity of Narragansett Avenue.
Mrs. Sheldon was the sister-in-law of H.A.C. Taylor, and the house
passed to the Taylor estate until its eventual demolition following World
War II.

## BEACH CLIFFE *(1852)*

*Oliver DeLancey Kane House*
*Detlef Lienau and Léon Marcotte, architects*
*Bath Road (now Memorial Boulevard)*
*between Annandale Road and Cliff Street*
*Demolished*

With Château-sur-Mer and Malbone, the DeLancey Kane estate Beach Cliffe was the most opulent of pre–Civil War Newport villas and the first modern French château in the city. The German-born, Paris-trained Lienau formed a partnership with the French-born, New York–based cabinetmaker/decorator Marcotte between 1850 and 1854. Beach Cliffe resulted from this collaboration, and with its French Second Empire facades and cosmopolitan Louis XV–style academic interiors was decades ahead of its time. DeLancey Kane and his wife, née Louisa Astor Langdon, were leaders of the Newport–New York social set, and Kane brought the first four-in-hand road coach, *Tallyho*, from England to America. The estate was sold in 1867 to the Philadelphia publisher Charles J. Peterson and later to Richard V. Mattison. In 1939, Eugene J. O'Reilly bought the property for $12,000 and subsequently demolished the main house to subdivide the property. Both the gate house (ca. 1859) by Newport architect Seth Bradford, facing Memorial Boulevard, and the carriage house (ca. 1895), on Annandale Road, however, survive.

Left: *Beach Cliffe, ca. 1875*

*Linden Gate, main facade* (top), *ca. 1880,*
*and garden facade* (bottom), *ca. 1897*

*Linden Gate, ca. 1947*

## HOUSE N<sup>o.</sup> 15

# LINDEN GATE *(1873)*
*Henry G. Marquand House*
*Richard Morris Hunt, architect*
*Rhode Island Avenue and Old Beach Road*
*Demolished*

Built as the summer residence of H.G. Marquand of New York, Linden Gate was a large picturesque cottage built of random-coursed ashlar, diamond-patterned red and black brick, and upper stories of half-timbering with intricate bargeboards. The interior featured a paneled room by Hunt's collaborator, the Florentine sculptor Luigi Frullini, and interior decoration by John La Farge and Samuel Colman. Mr. Marquand, railroad financier and philanthropist, was the president of the Board of Trustees of the Metropolitan Museum of Art, a long-time friend of Hunt, and an inveterate collector. So crammed with ceramics, textiles, and antiques were the interiors of Linden Gate that contemporaries labeled the house "Bric-a-Brac Hall." The property was maintained by Marquand's daughter and son-in-law, Mr. and Mrs. Roderick Terry, until sold by their estate in 1951. Converted to apartments and offices, the house was severely damaged by fire on February 18, 1973. Some reception room paneling, including elements by Frullini, was salvaged and Linden Gate was demolished for a residential subdivision.

*Linden Gate,
reception room,
ca. 1883*

ENTRANCE HALL

*Linden Gate,
hall,
ca. 1951*

*Pumpelly Cottage, ca. 1885*

## HOUSE N⁰· 16

## PUMPELLY COTTAGE *(1881)*
*Calvert Vaux, architect*
*Gibbs Avenue between Catherine and Francis Streets*
*Demolished*

This three-story stick-style chalet with Orientalist trim appeared every bit as exotic as Raphael Pumpelly, the successful geologist and explorer who commissioned it from his friend Vaux. With wide views from its verandas to Easton's Pond and the sea beyond, the house appeared like an exotic gypsy wagon on the heights of Gibbs Avenue. Following Pumpelly's death in 1923 the house was sold by his heirs in April 1924 to a neighbor, Julia W. Emmons, to be incorporated into her estate. The house, damaged by fire, was demolished and contemporary homes later built on the site.

*Pumpelly Cottage, street facade, ca. 1890*

HOUSE Nº· 17

LADD VILLA *(CA. 1865)*
*John G. Ladd, architect*
*Bath Road (now Memorial Boulevard)*
*Demolished*

Built by the architect John G. Ladd as his summer residence, this rambling timber-framed, cupola-clad Italianate villa was continually added to by the architect, as witnessed by the projecting ells. Set far back from Bath Road when this section of the city was regarded as highly desirable, the Ladd family continued in residence until 1910, when the surviving heir, Maude Ladd Scott, sold the house to Messrs. Hirsch and Hyman, Providence developers. With the then pending widening of Bath Road about to commence, plans were made to build bungalows on the grounds. On May 16,1911, fire ravaged the house. Plans to repair the structure were abandoned and in March of 1912 the property was sold to Rhode Island Senator George P. Wetmore for demolition; he acquired the land primarily to hasten the widening of Bath Road. The site was rezoned for twenty-four building lots, and the Memorial Boulevard frontage is now commercial.

Left: *Ladd Villa, street facade, ca. 1897*

MAP → OF
THE CITY OF
# NEWPORT
RHODE ISLAND
WITH PRINCIPAL POINTS OF INTEREST
AND SUMMER RESIDENCES WITH NAMES OF OWNERS

1937

# COTTAGES OF
# BELLEVUE AVENUE

Top: *Stone Villa, street facade, ca. 1957*
Bottom: *Stone Villa, watercolor of garden facade
by Mstislav Dobujinsky, 1949*

*Stone Villa, ca. 1920*

## HOUSE N⁰· 18

STONE VILLA *(CA. 1832–1835, ALTERATIONS CA. 1885)*
*Middleton, Brooks, Bennett, Whitehouse Estate*
*Alexander McGregor, Dudley Newton, architects*
*Bellevue Avenue between Jones Avenue and William Street*
*Demolished*

An impressive fieldstone and granite-trimmed Italianate manor house
built by Newport stonemason Alexander McGregor, Stone Villa was
significantly embellished by local architect Dudley Newton and the
firm of McIntosh & Alger for James Gordon Bennett, publisher of the
*New York Herald* and the *Paris Herald*. Bennett was responsible for the
installation of the gatepost owls, symbolic of the *New York Herald*. The
house had been a Newport landmark since the earlier days of such
occupants as the Middleton family of Charleston, South Carolina,
and the Brooks family of Boston. Later still it became associated with
Imperial Russia when leased by successive Russian ambassadors as the
summer legation and residence. The estate's final owner was William
F. Whitehouse of New York, from whose estate the property was acquired by developers in 1957 and demolished for the Bellevue Shopping
Center.

*Stone Villa, ca. 1955*

*Mrs. Paran Stevens Villa, ca. 1890*

## HOUSE N$^o$· 19

## PARAN STEVENS VILLA *(1866)*
*George Platt, architect*
*Bellevue Avenue at Jones Street*
*Demolished*

This lavish "steamboat gothic" villa was built for Mrs. Paran Stevens of New York, the energetic and socially ambitious widow of a hotel entrepreneur. Her daughter Mary became Lady Paget, a major London hostess. The family cottage sat to the rear of Stone Villa's block, on former Middleton family land, hidden from view by luxuriant evergreens and deciduous trees. The divorced 8th Duke of Marlborough was a summer guest of Mrs. Stevens in 1887 and embarked from here on his courtship of the wealthy American widow Lily Hamersley, later to become his duchess. The tactic would be repeated by his son the 9th Duke at Mrs. W.K. Vanderbilt's Marble House in Newport in 1895, Lady Paget serving, like her mother, as a marital agent. The house was demolished to extend the grounds of Stone Villa around 1925.

*Lady Paget
as Cleopatra,
1897,
Duke of Devonshire
Ball, London*

*Paran Stevens Villa,
ca. 1875*

*Arleigh, street facade, ca. 1910*

## HOUSE Nº. 20

### ARLEIGH *(1893)*
*Mrs. Ruthven H. Pratt Estate*
*J.D. Johnston, architect*
*Bellevue Avenue at Parker Avenue*
*Demolished*

Built by Mrs. Mary Matthews and her daughter Mrs. R.H. Pratt, this Queen Anne–style villa, incorporating elements from the earlier Deacon Cottage, was subsequently leased to Mrs. Potter Palmer of Chicago and to Isabel Gebhard Neilson of New York. It hosted the 1903 marriage of Cathleen Neilson to Reginald C. Vanderbilt. In the following years, the estate was occupied by the social arbiter Harry Symes Lehr and his wife, Elizabeth Drexel Dahlgren Lehr, and was the site of the Lehrs' witty "Dogs' Dinner," cohosted with Mrs. Stuyvesant Fish. Ravaged by arson on June 13, 1932, the house was torn down and a nursing home built on the site in 1972.

*Villa Rosa, entrance hall* (top),
*and dining room* (bottom),
*ca. 1904.*

*Villa Rosa, garden facade, ca. 1904*

## HOUSE N⁰· 21

## VILLA ROSA *(1901)*
*E. Rollins Morse–James Ben Ali Haggin Estate*
*Ogden Codman, architect*
*Bellevue Avenue between Dixon Street and Narragansett Avenue*
*Demolished*

Built as the summer residence of Mr. and Mrs. E. Rollins Morse of Boston and New York, Villa Rosa was amongst Codman's most successful country houses. Oriented to the south rather than east to the street, the house took maximum advantage of its long narrow setting. The gateposts led to a forecourt, followed by a walled inner court whose visual perspective from the street was terminated with a classical fountain set into a niche. The niche centered a trellis–decorated rear wing which was actually staff quarters, and the villa's neoclassical facade opened to the left onto the gravel courtyard. This plan was based on that of eighteenth–century French aristocratic townhouses and was unique in America in 1900. The exterior of the house was covered in pastel yellow stucco, later painted pink, offset with white bas–relief panels and was crowned by a copper dome. The lawn terminated at Narragansett Avenue with a circular marble gazebo copied from Marie Antoinette's Temple of Love (1778) by Richard Mique at Versailles.

*Villa Rosa trellised ballroom (the allegorical bas-relief plaster panels seen set into the trelliswork were salvaged and are now in the collections of Belcourt Castle, Newport), circa 1904*

*Villa Rosa garden facade with the Haggin children, circa 1915.*

Villa Rosa's interiors were equally impressive. A rigorous French classicism dominated, with white or white-and green paneled reception rooms. The heart of the house was the green trellised circular music room or ballroom, the first room in the United States to incorporate lattice design as a comprehensive decorative scheme. Subsequently occupied in 1913 by the James Ben Ali Haggin family of California, Kentucky, and New York, Villa Rosa was sold by the estate of its final occupant, Mrs. Emily Coddington Williams, on July 20, 1953, for $21,500 to E.A. McNulty, a Rhode Island contractor. Ogden Codman's

*Mrs. James Haggin, ca. 1915*

masterpiece was demolished in December of 1962 and a brick apartment complex (now condominiums) built on the site in 1965. Townhouse condominiums replaced the gardens in 1980 and the gateposts, one of the final vestiges, were cleared in 2004.

Above:
*Entrance gate and
forecourt,
ca. 1930*

Right:
*Courtyard
and entrance facade,
ca. 1904*

*George H. Warren House, ca. 1920*

## HOUSE N⁰· 22

### GEORGE HENRY WARREN HOUSE *(1861)*
*George Champlin Mason Sr., architect*
*Narragansett Avenue at Clay Street*
*Demolished*

Erected as part of Newport promoter and architect George Champlin Mason Sr.'s 1860 development of the Narragansett Avenue corridor, which included Mason-designed summer cottages for such prominent New York summer colonists as the Ogden, Schermerhorn, Tiffany, and Warren families, the George H. Warren house was typical of Mason construction. A large projecting wing with a single-story bay window was joined by a wraparound veranda to a central corps with an asymmetrical candle-snuffer-topped tower. The house was occupied by two generations of G.H. Warrens and sold by the family on September 20, 1921, to their neighbor to the east, Emily Morris (Mrs. R. Horace) Gallatin. Mrs. Gallatin promptly demolished the house to incorporate the site into the grounds of her property, Chepstow.

*Whitney Warren House, ca. 1920*

## HOUSE N°· 23

### WHITNEY WARREN HOUSE ( CA. 1860)
*Attributed to George Champlin Mason, architect*
*Clay Street at Parker Avenue*
*Demolished*

By 1885 George H. Warren Jr.'s younger brother, the budding architect Whitney Warren, had acquired the virtually neighboring Emily L.
Pennington cottage, attributed to Mason, for himself and his new bride,
Charlotte Tooker of Newport and New York, creating somewhat of a
family compound. Whitney Warren's estate would later sell the property
in 1943 to Newport real estate investor Eugene J. O'Reilly, who converted the house into apartments. Preferring not to see the family home
used in this manner, the heirs of Whitney Warren repurchased the property in 1955 and had the house demolished for residential subdivision.

*Right: Whiteholme, gates, ca. 1905*

Top: *Whiteholme, salon, ca. 1905*
Bottom: *Whiteholme, west wing, ca. 1905*

*Whiteholme, garden facade, ca. 1930*

## HOUSE N⁰. 24

## WHITEHOLME *(1901)*
*Mrs. Robert Garrett Estate*
*John Russell Pope, architect*
*Narragansett Avenue at Ochre Point Avenue*
*Demolished*

Built as the summer villa of Mary Frick Garrett (later Mrs. H. Barton Jacobs), the widow of Robert Garrett, president of the Baltimore and Ohio Railroad, Whiteholme was among the first residential commissions of the celebrated architect John Russell Pope. The architect placed a new French classical villa in front of and encasing the existing 1862 stick-style Thomas H. Hitchcock House. The Hitchcock House had been renovated by the architect Richard Morris Hunt, who added a ballroom, in 1869–1872, for William R. Travers. Working with the existing Hitchcock-Travers House, Pope created an unusual Gothic-shaped stucco-over-brick structure. The urbane French interiors were subcontracted to Allard & Sons of Paris and New York, and the formal statuary-filled garden was noted for its compact geometry. Whiteholme was sold in 1944 for $26,000 to its final private owner, Annette Townsend Phillips of Newport. Subsequently sold to Thomas P. Bilodeau, the estate was acquired by Salve Regina College on January 8, 1963, and was demolished in April 1963 for the construction of a modern student residence and dining facility. Donald Tinney of Newport acquired the painted and natural carved paneling from several reception rooms for the collection at Belcourt Castle, and a pair of allegorical statues from the garden were acquired by a Kansas City developer, J.C. Nichols, and moved to Prairie Village, Kansas.

*Whiteholme, garden facade, ca. 1905*

*Whiteholme, entrance facade, ca. 1945*

*Sulthorne, ca. 1970*

## HOUSE N⁰· 25

### SULTHORNE *(1847)*
*Lyman Estate*
*Architect unknown*
*Webster Street between Bellevue and Lawrence Avenues*
*Demolished*

This large white timber-framed mid-nineteenth-century Victorian cottage was built for Charles Lyman of Boston and remained in his family until the 1973 death of Cyril B. Judge, widower of the former Annie Lyman. The house was demolished that year and the grounds used as open space by Mrs. Elinor Dorrance Hill Ingersoll, owner of a nearby estate. The property has since been sold by her heirs and is now subdivided for luxury homes; slightly over one acre however was preserved as open space with conservation easements in 2009.

*From the Gustave J.S. White auction catalog, July 1973*

*Greystone, north facade, ca. 1890*

*Greystone, south facade, ca. 1890*

*Greystone, gates, ca. 1890*

## HOUSE Nº. 26

### GREYSTONE *(1883)*
*Bosworth-Wysong-Jelke Estate*
*George Champlin Mason, architect*
*Ochre Point Avenue between Victoria and Ruggles Avenues*
*Demolished*

The aptly named Greystone was a roughhewn granite Romanesque revival villa built for Fitch Bosworth in 1883 by local architects George Champlin Mason & Son and sold in 1887 to John Jelke Wysong. The interiors were noted for a stained glass program designed by Donald MacDonald for William McPherson & Co. of Boston, and the house was significantly renovated by Newport architect J.D. Johnston in 1889. The estate was last owned by Mr. John F. Jelke Jr. when destroyed by arson during the evening of May 31, 1938. The gateposts and boundary wall survive but the site is now the visitor parking lot of The Breakers, directly opposite.

Top: *The Cloister, garden facade, ca. 1930*
Bottom: *The Cloister, street facade, ca. 1930*

*The Cloister, gates, ca. 1930*

HOUSE N°· 27

## THE CLOISTER *(1887)*

*John Dixon Johnston, architect; alterations by Delano & Aldrich*
*Ruggles Avenue at Wetmore Avenue*
*Demolished*

The Cloister was built as a timber-framed guest cottage with a large round-arched granite post veranda that gave the house its name. Originally the property of Catherine Lorillard Kernochan, whose villa stood next door, the house was acquired by New York financier William Woodward and his wife, Elsie Cryder Woodward, around 1910. The Woodwards embarked on a major renovation campaign with the architectural firm of Delano & Aldrich that was completed by 1914. The resultant shingle-style house was demolished in 1950 and the site later subdivided for contemporary homes.

## D'HAUTEVILLE COTTAGE *(1871)*
*Peabody & Stearns, architects*
*Bellevue Avenue between Gordon Street and Victoria Avenue*
*Demolished*

A fanciful stick-style and half-timbered cottage, this house was designed as one of the first residential commissions of the architectural firm of Peabody & Stearns, for F.S.G. d'Hauteville of Switzerland and Boston. The cottage was acquired in 1929 by Francis Saxhaw Elwes Drury of London, who had married Mabel Gerry of Newport and New York. Rebaptized Drury Lodge, the house remained in the Drury family into the 1950s, when, following a fire, it was largely razed. A truncated fragment of the house remains.

Left: *D'Hauteville Cottage, ca. 1875*

*Stoneacre, street facade, ca. 1930*

## HOUSE N<sup>o.</sup> 29

## STONEACRE *(1882)*
*Ellis-Loew Estate*
*William Appleton Potter, architect*
*Bellevue Avenue between Victoria and Ruggles Avenues*
*Demolished*

This vast shingle-style cottage, with a broad front piazza and exotic dome overlooking grounds designed by Frederick Law Olmsted, was built for John W. Ellis, founder of the First National Bank in Cincinnati and a director of the Northern Pacific Railroad. Sold to E.R. and Linda Thomas, the estate was acquired in 1916 and renovated by William Goadby and Florence Baker Loew of New York. The Loew family sold Stoneacre in 1955 to Gustave Pierre Bader for $24,500. Bader, in 1957, transferred ownership to the Hatch Preparatory School and the property became, with a half-dozen estates along central Bellevue Avenue, a dormitory first for the Hatch School and later for Vernon Court Junior College. Demolished in 1962 for a planned academic building and recreational campus, these new construction plans were canceled by the 1973 bankruptcy of the school. While the other former estate dormitories were developed into condominiums, the site of Stoneacre remained empty and is now preserved as the Frederick Law Olmsted Park. The surviving stable building was saved by conversion into condominiums in 1986 and is now a student residence for Salve Regina University.

*Chetwode, aerial view, ca. 1935*

*Chetwode, garden fountain, ca. 1910*

*Chetwode, garden facade, ca. 1910*

## HOUSE N⁰. 30

### CHETWODE *(1903)*
*Storrs Wells–Astor Estate*
*Horace Trumbauer, architect*
*Bellevue Avenue between Victoria and Ruggles Avenues*
*Demolished*

A limestone-trimmed brick Louis XIV–style château, Chetwode was built for Mrs. William Storrs Wells (née Annie Raynor) of New York by the Philadelphia architect Horace Trumbauer. With formal landscaping by the architect John Russell Pope and opulent interior reception rooms by Allard & Sons, decorators, of Paris and New York, Chetwode became one of the most lavish villas ever erected in Newport. The white-and -gold paneled salons were in Louis XV and Louis XVI taste based on the king's private apartments at Versailles. The dining room, library, and morning room contained Old Master paintings set into the wall decoration. Occupied by Mrs. Wells until the 1930 season, the estate was then leased to A.J. Drexel Biddle Jr. for three years and then sold, largely furnished, on January 23, 1934, to John Jacob Astor III for $150,000. The estate comprised a garage-stable block, gardener's cottage, greenhouse, five acres of formal gardens, and grounds extending beyond Coggeshall

Avenue west to Carroll Avenue. The twenty-one-year-old Astor heir had just come of age and was soon to marry Miss Ellen Tuck French. Doris Duke Cromwell sublet Chetwode from the Astors for the 1937 season.

Five years after divorcing, the J. J. Astors placed the estate and contents on the auction block, and it sold in October of 1948 for $70,000 to James C. O'Donnell, a Washington investor. His daughter, Mrs. Florence O'Donnell Maher, sold the estate to the Texas-based Church of Christ for $45,000 in 1954, for use as a church and center for servicemen. In June of 1957, the church sold Chetwode for $40,000 to Thomas Diab and John P. Curran, Boston developers, for conversion into apartments. Finally, in November of 1958 the estate was sold, again for $40,000, to Miss Phoebe Warren Andrews of New York who, as president of the Newport Art League, held exhibitions and sponsored an art school in the house. During the morning of January 29, 1972, a chimney fire spread through the three floors of the villa causing devastating damage. Although retrievable, the house was

*Chetwode, hall chimneypiece, ca. 1910*

not restored and its interiors were sold off. The French paneling and mantels of the reception rooms are known to have been salvaged by the Tinney family and others, and are today dispersed between shops, restaurants, and private collections in Newport, Boston, New Jersey, and Paris. Chetwode, one of the chief glories of Newport, was razed in May of 1973. The outlying acreage from Ruggles to Carroll Avenues had become, after 1948, the setting for multiple residential subdivisions. The remaining five acres of gardens sold in August of 1976 for $96,000 for development into a six-lot subdivision, and the surviving stable-garage building was converted into condominiums.

*Chetwode, dining room, ca. 1930*

*Chetwode, grand salon, ca. 1930*

Top: *Chetwode, library, ca. 1930*
Bottom: *Chetwode, hall, ca. 1930*

Top: *Chetwode, petit salon, ca. 1930*
Bottom: *Chetwode, red drawing room, ca. 1930*

*Mrs. August Belmont,*
*ca. 1870*

*Mrs. Belmont in her* demi d'Aumont *carriage, ca. 1870*

*By-the-Sea, ca. 1875*

## HOUSE Nº· 31

## BY-THE-SEA *(1860)*
*Belmont Estate*
*George Champlin Mason Sr., architect; alterations by Horace Trumbauer*
*Bellevue Avenue at Marine Avenue*
*Demolished*

Due to family ties that united the Perry and Champlin families in Newport, George Champlin Mason's fledgling architectural practice was assured when launched in 1860 with the commission for the August Belmont villa, By-the-Sea. The commission was received through Mrs. Belmont, née Caroline Perry, a daughter of Commodore Matthew Perry. Mr. Belmont began his career in New York as the Rothschild family's American representative. Summering in her native Newport, Mrs. Belmont introduced the Rothschild penchant for things French, from liveried footmen to a celebrated *"demi d'Aumont"* carriage, to the summer colony. The house was classic early Mason: an Italianate cottage with mansard roof, a three-bay entrance front pavilion, and conventional bracketed trim. By-the-Sea was updated considerably during the classicizing alterations undertaken by Horace Trumbauer, in 1910 for Mr. Belmont's son Perry Belmont of

Top: *By-the-Sea, garden facade, ca. 1930*
Bottom: *By-the-Sea, salon, ca. 1910*

Washington, D.C. Sold out of the family by his estate, By-the-Sea became a rental property and the legendary summer home of Washington-based socialite Evalyn Walsh MacLean. The property was subsequently sold for delinquent taxes from the 44 East 34th Street Corporation to James C. O'Donnell, who promptly resold to Ray Alan Van Clief, the then-owner of Rosecliff, the abutting former Oelrichs estate. Mr. Van Clief demolished By-the-Sea in 1946 to join its lands with those of Rosecliff. Following Van Clief's sudden death, the Belmont and Oelrichs estates were jointly sold in 1947 to J. Edgar Monroe of New Orleans, who in 1971 donated the combined properties to the Preservation Society. Twelve acres, comprising the bulk of the fourteen acres of the former By-the-Sea property, were soon thereafter sold to a land investment company and proceeds placed in an endowment for Rosecliff. The estate grounds were subdivided and modern homes built on the site beginning in 1986.

*W. W. Tucker House, ca. 1875*

HOUSE Nº· 32

## W.W. TUCKER HOUSE *(1869)*
*Tucker-Post Estate*
*George Champlin Mason, architect; alterations by J.D. Johnston*
*Bellevue Avenue facing Marine Avenue*
*Demolished*

The William W. Tucker family of Boston chose Newport architect George Champlin Mason to build their Italianate cottage near the cliffs at the end of Bellevue Avenue overlooking a chasm that inspired the estate's name, The Grotto. The views appealed to the Vanderbilt brothers. From 1881 until his purchase of the former Lorillard estate in 1885, Cornelius Vanderbilt II sublet the Tucker cottage every season. His younger brother, Frederick W. Vanderbilt, subsequently acquired the Tucker property and began construction on the more palatial Rough Point in 1888. He had the timber-framed Tucker house moved to a new site down Bellevue Avenue and renovated by J.D. Johnston. The cottage was then presented to the Post family, Mrs. Post being a sister of Mrs. Frederick W. Vanderbilt, née Louise Anthony. The house in turn passed to Margaret

Louise Post, the future Mrs. James L. Van Alen and later still Mrs. Louis Bruguiere. Rebaptized Rosetta Villa, the house was sold by Mrs. Bruguiere to Newport real estate developer James T. O'Connell, who razed the villa in 1938. The site was subsequently part of the Vernon Court Junior College complex and was sold as a vacant residential lot in 2004. A sizable new French manor house now occupies the site.

*Hawthorne Villa, ca. 1910*

## HOUSE N⁰. 33

## HAWTHORNE VILLA *(1860)*
*Stevenson Estate*
*Architect unknown*
*Carroll and Bateman Avenues*
*Demolished*

A large Gothic revival fieldstone cottage built for J.B. Smith, sold to the Arnold family, and long occupied by the Stevenson family of Philadelphia, Hawthorne Villa was set far back on its lot in an English Romantic landscape. This served as the demarcation line between the urban residential fifth ward and the estate district. The villa was demolished in 1967 for a naval housing complex known as Newport Manor, which has recently been privatized as condominiums.

*The Reefs, garden facade, ca. 1875*

*The Reefs (Whitney Cottage), dining room, ca. 1898*

*The Reefs, street facade, ca. 1857*

## HOUSE N⁰· 34

## THE REEFS *(1853)* – WHITNEY COTTAGE
*Wolfe-Knower-Whitney Estate*
*Joseph Wells, architect; alterations by Ogden Codman*
*Bellevue Avenue at Bancroft Avenue*
*Demolished*

Built for Christopher Wolfe of New York, this fine Italianate villa was one of the pre–Civil War showplaces of Newport. Sold to T.W. Phinney in 1858, it was subsequently purchased by John Knower of New York. His cousin, Sarah French, sold the estate to Mr. and Mrs. Harry Payne Whitney (née Gertrude Vanderbilt) in 1896. The Reefs was then encased in stucco and renovated by the architect Ogden Codman as Whitney Cottage. Gertrude Vanderbilt Whitney added a shingle-style sculpture studio on the cliffs, where she studied under the tutelage of Hendrik Christian Andersen. This studio was swept away in the great hurricane that devastated the southern New England coast on September 21, 1938. It was replaced with a yellow brick *moderne*-style version by Noel and Miller, architects, in 1939. In December of 1942, while occupied by the family of Mrs. Whitney's sister, Countess Laszlo Széchényi, the villa caught fire. The main structure was demolished in 1945, the surviving gatehouse was sold and moved to nearby Ruggles Avenue, and the site acquired by Mr. S. Griswold Flagg of Radnor, Pennsylvania. The Flagg family in turn sold the estate, with Gertrude Whitney's surviving studio, to Reginald Rives, who in 1953 had a Georgian-style red brick house built on the lower slope of the lot by architect Frederick Rhinelander King.

Top: *The Reefs (Whitney Cottage), entrance facade, ca. 1930;* Bottom: *garden facade, ca. 193.*

*Reef Point, entrance facade, ca. 1890*

ℓ

## HOUSE Nᵒ· 35

## REEF POINT *(1865)*
*Yznaga-Ingersoll-Carson Estate*
*Architect unknown*
*Yznaga Avenue and the Cliffs*
*Demolished*

This ambitious Italianate timber-framed villa was built for Cuban-American planter Antonio Yznaga del Valle of Louisiana, in whose honor the small private street off the east side of Bellevue Avenue was named. Yznaga's daughter Consuelo was a childhood friend of Alva Erskine Smith, subsequently Mrs. William K. Vanderbilt, who spent much time in this cottage as a girl. Alva Vanderbilt's sister Mary Virginia Smith married Consuelo's brother Fernando, and Alva's daughter was named in her honor following Consuelo's aristocratic marriage to Viscount Mandeville, later Duke of Manchester.

The estate passed to Harry Ingersoll and subsequently to Robert N. Carson, a retired Philadelphia banker. Following the 1904 construction of the Edward C. Knight Jr. estate, Clarendon Court, on the Bellevue Avenue frontage of Yznaga Avenue, Reef Point was purchased by Mr. Knight in February of 1910 to extend the grounds of his estate to the cliffs. The house was pulled down to extend the vista to the sea and its site landscaped into the Clarendon Court property.

*Gull Rock, aerial view, ca. 1955*

## HOUSE Nº· 36

## GULL ROCK *(1870)*
*McKim-Hunnewell Estate*
*Dudley Newton, architect*
*Bellevue and Yznaga Avenues*
*Demolished*

Built in 1870 as the summer residence of Robert V. McKim, Gull Rock, a rambling Queen Anne–style cottage perched on the edge of the cliffs, was sold in 1876 to Hollis Hunnewell of Boston, who undertook major alterations with his architect, George Russell Shaw, in 1883. The estate was subsequently owned by Robert Gould Shaw of Boston, then by Mr. A. L. Humes of New York, and lastly by E. Bruce Merriman of Providence. Acquired in November 1972 by Mr. and Mrs. Claus von Bulow, Gull Rock was demolished and its site incorporated into the grounds of adjacent Clarendon Court. Following the 1988 sale of the von Bulow estate, the Gull Rock site was separated and sold as the setting for a contemporary home.

Top: *Seaverge, (right) aerial, and Rockhurst (left), ca. 1930*
Middle: *Seaverge, garden facade, ca. 1955*
Bottom: *Seaverge, entrance facade, ca. 1955*

*Seaverge, salon, ca. 1955*

## HOUSE N⁰· 37

SEAVERGE *(CA. 1855)*
*Gerry-Hartford Estate*
*Original architect unknown; alterations by Peabody & Stearns*
*Bellevue Avenue at curve*
*Demolished*

A large midnineteenth-century timber-framed cottage built for John Paine of New York, Seaverge was much altered and embellished by Henry H. Cook in 1883 using the Boston architectural firm of Peabody & Stearns. The estate, again enlarged, subsequently became the summer home of Elbridge T. Gerry of New York, the celebrated yachtsman, and subsequently in 1927 of Mrs. Edward V. Hartford and later Mrs. Peyton van Rensselaer. In 1955, Seaverge was acquired by the Harold B. Tinneys, who lived there until their purchase in 1956 for $25,000 of nearby Belcourt. Seaverge was sold and in 1957 demolished for subdivision. The Tinney family salvaged significant interior architectural elements for their collection, together with a seahorse weathervane which now tops the stable block at Belcourt.

*Rockhurst, garden facade, ca. 1923*

*Rockhurst, gate lodge, ca. 1898*

## HOUSE Nº· 38

### ROCKHURST *(1891)*
*H. Mortimer Brooks Estate*
*Peabody & Stearns, architects*
*Bellevue Avenue and Ledge Road*
*Demolished*

This stone-and-shingle summer residence for Mrs. H. Mortimer Brooks of New York was amongst the most château-esque of Peabody & Stearns's Newport cottages. The street facade featured rounded towers with candle-snuffer roofs flanking a central block with an open arcaded gallery along the second story. The garden elevation faced the sea with a broad central veranda. Following Mrs. Brooks's death in 1920, the estate was sold to the John Aspegrens, who renamed the property Aspen Hall during their 1922–29 occupancy. In 1930, the estate was purchased by Mrs. Walter B. James of New York and, in 1944, by Frederick H. Prince, who had purchased the nearby Marble House in 1932 for $1 (excluding furnishings). Mr. Prince sold Rockhurst, then called Lowlands, in 1945 to a real estate syndicate headed by Charles G. West, which chose to demolish the main house in September of 1955 for residential subdivision. The gatehouse and gardener's cottage survive and, recently restored by Mr. West's descendants, give an excellent idea of the scale of the Brooks villa.

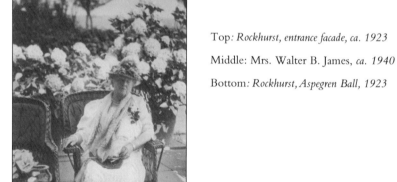

Top: *Rockhurst, entrance facade, ca. 1923*

Middle: Mrs. Walter B. James, *ca. 1940*

Bottom: *Rockhurst, Aspegren Ball, 1923*

*Train Villa (Beachholm), ca. 1890*

## HOUSE №· 39

### BEACHHOLM *(1869)*
*G. F. Train Estate*
*Cyrus Peckham, builder*
*Bellevue Avenue at Bailey's Beach*
*Demolished*

Formerly known as the Train Villa, this was considered the last large mansard Italianate cottage erected in Newport. Built for George F. Train of Boston, the estate was subsequently acquired by Newport real estate promoter Alfred Smith and later by Woodbury Blair of New York. Badly damaged by fire in the early 1970s, it was replaced with a contemporary home on the site.

*Train Villa (Beachholm), ca. 1920*

*Train Villa (Beachholm), ca. 1947*

*Richard Baker House, aerial view, ca. 1925*

HOUSE N°· 40

## RICHARD BAKER JR. HOUSE, WESTCLIFF *(1870)*
*Richard Morris Hunt, architect*
*Ledge Road*
*Demolished*

Characteristic of Hunt's early Newport cottages, the Baker House, visible in these rare views, was a large asymmetrically planned stick-style cottage with picturesque verandas and balconies reminiscent of his 1863 Griswold House in Newport. Here, however, Hunt renovating an existing 1854 cottage built for Charles Mixter, adding contrasting rooflines. These consisted of hipped and gambrel roofs giving way to high-pitched mansard towers, which while remaining timber-framed were to be a signal of the architect's evolution toward the chateau-esque. Sold in 1923 by the Richard Baker Jr. estate to Dr. Truman L. Saunders of New York, the house was pulled down and replaced with a "Normandy manor"–style residence.

*Baker Cottage seen from Bailey's Beach 1919*

*Cadwalader Cottage, ca. 1925*

## HOUSE N°· 41

### CADWALADER COTTAGE *(1853)*
*T.D. Spooner, builder*
*Bellevue Avenue at Ledge Road*
*Demolished*

On land acquired in 1852 from Newport real estate speculator Joseph I. Bailey, General George Cadwalader of Philadelphia had Newport builder T.D. Spooner erect in 1853 a large, square, timber-framed Victorian cottage. Set in a parklike setting designed by Newport landscape architect Thomas Galvin, the villa remained in the Cadwalader family through the midtwentieth century. Major renovations were undertaken in 1889 under the direction of Newport architect J.D. Johnston. Sold on September 5, 1942, to Mrs. Fannie Magnin, the house was demolished following a fire in the following decade. The site was sold in September 1961 to Martha Wadsworth and is now occupied by a contemporary villa known as Tree Haven by architect George Henry Warren.

MAP → OF
THE CITY OF
# NEWPORT
## RHODE ISLAND
WITH PRINCIPAL POINTS OF INTEREST
AND SUMMER RESIDENCES WITH NAMES OF OWNERS

1937

# COTTAGES OF
# OCEAN AVENUE

*The Rocks, seaside facade, ca. 1890*

*The Rocks, entrance facade, ca. 1930*

*The Rocks, entrance facade, ca. 1920*

*The Rocks, seen from Bailey's Beach, 1938*

## HOUSE N<sup>o.</sup> 42

## THE ROCKS *(1868)*
*Boit-Clews Estate*
*John Hubbard Sturgis, architect*
*Ocean Avenue (west of Bailey's Beach)*
*Demolished*

Built by Boston architects Russell & Sturgis for the Boston artist Edward Darley Boit and his wife, Mary Louisa Cushing Boit, The Rocks was a rambling timber and granite Queen Anne villa sited on land belonging to Mrs. Boit's family. Following the Boits' departure for Paris, The Rocks was acquired first by Robert B. Potter and then by Thomas J. Montgomery, and by 1890 it was the summer estate of New York banker Henry Clews. The dramatic setting of the house, melting into a boulder-strewn field overlooking the famed Spouting Rock, inspired the artistic aspirations of Henry Clews Jr., who became a noted sculptor. The house, encased in stucco and much added on to by the Clews family, was demolished in 1948 following the May 1945 sale of the property by Mr. Clews's estate and its grounds incorporated back into the adjoining Cushing property.

# HOUSE № 43

## SEAFIELD (CA. 1853)
Harper-Field-Warren Estate
Thomas Alexander Tefft, architect
Ocean Avenue at Jeffrey Road
Demolished

Miss Emily Harper, granddaughter of Charles Carroll of Baltimore, commissioned a mansard-roof cottage with continuously shingled walls and roof from the then popular Providence architect Thomas Tefft. The same year, Miss Harper and her mother provided most of the money to erect St. Mary's Church in Newport by the architect Patrick C. Keely. The house was subsequently sold to John N.A. Griswold and then to John M. Fields of Philadelphia. Fields much enlarged the cottage and rebaptized it Seafields, a name later shortened to Seafield. The George Henry Warrens of New York subsequently owned the property through World War II. Following the war, the house was acquired by a Newport real estate syndicate and leased seasonally; its last occupants were the owners, crew, families, and staff of the British challenging yacht for the America's Cup, the *Sovereign*, in 1964. Known popularly as "Mildew Manor" by these tenants, Seafield was sold in 1965 to Howard G. Cushing, owner of the adjacent estate, and demolished in 1966. The land has since been split off again and a new house was built on the site in 2000.

Top: *Beacon Hill House, entrance facade, ca. 1937*
Center: *Beacon Hill House, aerial view, ca. 1947*
Bottom: *Beacon Hill House, hall, ca. 1912*

*Beacon Hill House, ca. 1912*

HOUSE N⁰· 44

## BEACON HILL HOUSE *(1910)*
*Arthur Curtiss James Estate*
*Howells & Stokes, architects*
*Beacon Hill Road*
*Demolished*

Occupying the highest, rockiest hill of Newport, Beacon Hill House, named for the beacons that were once lit near its crest, was designed to blend into its natural environment in keeping with F. L. Olmsted's, H. H. Richardson's, and R. M. Hunt's recommendations for the development of this sector of Newport. When Mr. James acquired the property in 1909 an existing McKim, Mead & White fieldstone house known as Belvoir (J.E. Addicks residence) stood on the site and served as inspiration for the new, enlarged villa. Built of native gray puddingstone, the exterior of Beacon Hill House was relatively austere. The interiors, however, included fully paneled walnut reception rooms in Louis XVI and Jacobean taste and the *"della Robbia"* room, with a fountain and vaulted ceiling of Guastavino tiles. Mr. James was commodore of the New York Yacht Club, heir to the Phelps-Dodge copper mining interests, and a major western railroad investor.

His estate was the largest in Newport, at 125 acres, with three villas, a "Swiss village" model farm, elaborate formal gardens used for Mrs. James's musicales, and a harbor-front boathouse. With the deaths of Mr. and Mrs. James within three weeks of each other in 1941, the estate was willed to a foundation which, in 1951 after ten years of vandalism, gifted the houses and real estate to the Roman Catholic Diocese of Providence. One of the villas, Zeerust, was converted to a convent and novitiate, and a service building was made into an elementary school. The main house was seldom utilized and, in May of 1967, vandals started a fire in Beacon Hill House. Gutted, the estate was demolished in August of 1967 and 70 acres were sold for residential development. A fieldstone gatehouse and carriage house–garage survive as private residences.

*Beacon Hill House, seen from the Blue Garden, ca. 1920*

Top:
*Beacon Hill House,
living room,
ca. 1912*

Center:
*Beacon Hill House,
"della Robbia" room,
ca. 1912*

Bottom:
*Beacon Hill House,
drawing room,
ca. 1912*

Top: *The Reef, ca. 1890*
Center: *The Reef, garden, ca. 1914*
Bottom: *The Reef, ca. 1920*

*The Reef, ca. 1920*

## HOUSE N⁰· 45

### THE REEF *(1883)*
*T.M. Davis–Budlong Estate*
*John Hubbard Sturgis, architect*
*Ocean Avenue at Brenton's Point*
*Demolished*

The Reef was built at the southernmost tip of Aquidneck Island by Theodore M. Davis, copper magnate, author, collector, and renowned Egyptologist. The Boston architectural firm of Sturgis & Brigham created an elegant shingle-and-stone-clad Queen Anne villa destined to house Davis's collection of Old Master paintings, largely bought through the art consultant Bernard Berenson and later bequeathed to the Metropolitan Museum of Art in New York. Richly paneled reception rooms in Jacobean taste were hung with the painting collection, and the walled gardens and greenhouses were renowned. Between 1903 and 1912, T.M. Davis wintered on the Nile and was granted a license to dig from the Egyptian government. He discovered the tombs of Queen Hatshepsut, Tuthmosis IV, Siptah, Horemheb, Yuaa, and Thuiu, whose artifacts are now in the collections of the Cairo Museum.

Following Mr. Davis's death in 1915, the eighteen-acre estate was purchased by Mr. and Mrs. Milton J. Budlong of Providence. The Budlongs divorced in 1928 and the property was placed in contention. The house, never again lived in by the family, passed to Miss Frances Budlong. During World War II, antiaircraft gun emplacements were set up around the estate, which housed gunnery personnel. Vandalized throughout the 1950s, the villa became a popular romantic ruin and was set on fire in 1961. Demolished on May 25, 1963, the site is today a state park with a restored Davis-era bungalow and a now-derelict carriage house–stable built by the architect Theodore Davis Boal of Washington, D.C.

Top:
*The Reef, hall,
ca. 1928*

Bottom:
*The Reef,
drawing room,
ca. 1928*

*Bleak House, ca. 1897*

## HOUSE Nº· 46

## BLEAK HOUSE *(1895)*
*Winans-Perry Estate*
*Peabody & Stearns, architects; alterations by Stone & Carpenter*
*Ocean Avenue at Winans Avenue*
*Demolished*

Ross R. Winans, son of Baltimore railroad investor Thomas Winans, chose Peabody & Stearns to erect a low-slung shingle-style villa on an exposed ledge facing Pirate's Cove. Named after Dickens's novel, to continue the tradition of his father's so-named adjoining 1873 cottage by R.M. Hunt (demolished in 1894), Bleak House was sold to Providence utilities magnate Marsden J. Perry in 1907. The estate remained in the Perry family until badly damaged by the 1938 hurricane. The house was demolished in 1948 with salvaged stonework removed by Trappist monks for use in the construction of a new monastery in Spencer, Massachusetts. In 1949, the oceanfront site and service buildings across Ocean Avenue were sold to Newport developer Louis Chartier for $90,000, and a residential subdivision was begun facing the house's now open, exposed site.

*Bleak House, gates, ca. 1920*

*Bleak House, cliff side, ca. 1920*

*Bateman's Hotel, veranda, ca. 1930*

## HOUSE N⁰· 47

### BATEMAN'S *(CA. 1755)*
*Bateman-Davis Estate*
*Architect unknown*
*Commonwealth Avenue*
*Demolished*

A large mideighteenth-century country estate built for the prominent
Collins family of Newport was acquired in the 1840s by Seth Bateman, who by 1860 encased the original house in additions and operated
it as Bateman's Hotel. A favorite excursion spot for coaching meets,
formal picnics, and rustic dances, Bateman's became synonymous with
the Newport summer colony's lifestyle. Set back from the road in an
old orchard, the grounds were renowned for their picturesque quality,
which included a full-scale replica of the Old Stone Mill in Newport's
Touro Park. Acquired around 1893 by Edmund W. Davis, the property
was sold only in 1947 to Newport preservationist John Perkins Brown.

*Bateman's Hotel, aerial view, ca. 1930*

With funding provided by the Misses Wetmore of Château-sur-Mer and others, a restoration was planned to return the Bateman Hotel complex back to its eighteenth-century core. J. Perkins Brown, however, sold the property before work was much advanced to local developer Louis Chartier for $13,000 in 1957. The Bateman Hotel burned mysteriously on February 24, 1959, and the ruins were cleared for the Chartier subdivisions.

*Sunset Ridge, ca. 1888*

## HOUSE N<sup>o.</sup> 48

### SUNSET RIDGE *(1877)*
*Low-Ledyard Estate*
*George Champlin Mason, architect*
*Ridge Road*
*Demolished*

Built by the very social cottage architect George Champlin Mason, Sunset Ridge was the residence of prominent retired China trade merchant Abiel Abbot Low, founder of A.A. Low & Bros. of New York. Set at the top of a ridge overlooking the East Passage of Narragansett Bay, the house's broad west-facing veranda provided romantic views. Inherited by Seth Low, president of Columbia University, former mayor of Brooklyn, and second mayor of greater New York City (1901–03), the estate remained in the family until its purchase by Lewis Cass Ledyard of New York in 1905. The property was eventually joined with that of Broadlawns, built in 1866 for A.A. Low's brother Josiah Orne Low, to the south. To reduce tax valuations, Sunset Ridge was demolished in 1955.

Top: *Armsea Hall, garden facade, ca. 1914*

Center: *Armsea Hall, harbor view, ca. 1914*

Bottom: *Armsea Hall, aerial view, ca. 1955*

*Armsea Hall, garden facade, ca. 1940*

## HOUSE N⁰· 49

## ARMSEA HALL *(1901)*
*Greene-Hoffman-Johnson Estate*
*F.L.V. Hoppin, architect*
*Ridge Road*
*Demolished*

A large porticoed Palladian villa dominating the lower East Passage of Narragansett Bay, Armsea Hall was New York architect Francis Laurens Vinton Hoppin's Beaux-Arts masterpiece in Newport. Designed for General Francis Vinton Greene, the villa's neoclassical central core was flanked by two lower projecting wings with Doric colonnades. The estate, with its noted rose gardens and landscaping by Olmsted Brothers, passed within two years of construction to Charles Frederick Hoffman and then to Zelia K. Hoffman. Subsequently acquired in 1945 by Mrs. Aymar Johnson for $14,000, and later by Barclay Douglas, this palatial estate, abutting the Auchincloss family's Hammersmith Farm, childhood summer home of Jacqueline Bouvier Kennedy, was proposed as the official summer White House in 1962. President

Kennedy intended to privately lease the estate for his planned 1964 summer season. His assassination precluded occupancy and Armsea Hall was sold in 1965 for $150,000 for conversion to a resort. In 1967, the property was purchased at a mortgagee sale for $195,000 and in 1968 was sold a final time for $212,000 for a residential subdivision. The villa was demolished in 1969 and a modern home subsequently built on a portion of the property; the site of the main house remains open space.

*Armsea Hall, hydrangea walk, 1914*

*Vedimar, ca. 1930*

## HOUSE Nº. 50

### VEDIMAR *(1910)*
*Arthur Curtiss James Estate*
*Atterbury & Phelps, architects*
*Harrison Avenue*
*Demolished*

Set atop a rocky outcropping at the end of a long entrance drive, Vedimar was a stucco-over-timber-frame, Spanish-colonial-style villa built as a guest residence for Commodore Arthur Curtiss James's adjoining estate. Long occupied by Dr. Lewis F. Frissell, the property was sold by the James estate and remained private until the 1970s. Following auction of its contents, Vedimar was demolished in 1975 for institutional development of the site. That institution went into receivership and the resultant clinic buildings and parking lots were removed by a private Newport preservationist in 1999.

*Vedimar, living room, 1974*

*Vedimar, dining room, 1974*

*Pen Craig, entrance facade, ca. 1930*

## HOUSE N⁰· 51

### PEN CRAIG *(1865)*
*Jones-Webster Estate*
*Architect unknown*
*Harrison Avenue*
*Demolished*

Pen Craig was built as an informal timber-framed summer cottage over-looking Newport Harbor by Mr. and Mrs. George F. Jones, parents of the author Edith Wharton, who spent her formative childhood summers here. Just prior to 1900, the property was acquired by Mr. and Mrs. Hamilton Fish Webster of New York who "Tudorized" the cottage. Following the death of Mr. and Mrs. Webster, the house was sold at auction on July 17, 1956, to a group of local real estate investors, and Pen Craig was demolished for residential subdivision. A circa-1900 brick and clapboard carriage house survives.

*Harbourview, garden facade, ca. 1897*

*Harbourview, ca. 1910*

## HOUSE Nº· 52

HARBOURVIEW *(1865)*
*Merrill-French Estate*
*George Champlin Mason, architect*
*Wellington Avenue at Ida Lewis Yacht Club*
*Demolished*

Built for Ayres P. Merrill of Natchez by the active Newport architect George Champlin Mason, Harbourview was one of the most ambitious of Mason's Italianate cottages and was renovated by him for two subsequent owners. In 1870, the house was acquired by the New York collector Stephen Whitney Phoenix. Following Mr. Phoenix's death in 1881, the property was sold to New York lawyer and banker Francis Ormond French; his daughter Ellen Tuck French married Alfred Gwynne Vanderbilt in Newport in 1901, and their son, William H. Vanderbilt III, later became governor of Rhode Island. Following her divorce from A.G. Vanderbilt, Ellen Tuck French married Paul Fitzsimmons and resided at Harbourview until her own death there in 1948. Governor W.H. Vanderbilt sold the estate in 1951 and the house was demolished for residential subdivision.

# NOTES

UNPUBLISHED SOURCES:

Archives of The Preservation Society of Newport County,
424 Bellevue Avenue, Newport, R.I. 02840

Land Evidence Records of Newport, R.I.,
City Hall, Broadway, Newport, R.I. 02840

*New York Times* Archives

*Newport Daily News* Archives,
Malbone Road, Newport, R.I. 02840


PUBLISHED SOURCES:

Amory, Cleveland. "The Crucial Battle of Modern Newport,"
*New York Times Magazine,* 2 September 1962, pp. 128–30.

*Annuaire of the Newport Garden Club,* 1914, privately published,
Newport, R.I., 1915.

*Architecture,* Vol. XIV, No. 6, December 1906.

"Country Houses & Gardens," *The Spur,* 15 November, 1919.

*Fifty Glimpses of Newport,* Rand, McNally & Co.,
New York, 1897.

James, Henry. *The American Scene,* Harper & Brothers,
New York, 1907.

"Life Visits a Fading Newport," *Life* magazine, 16 October 1944.

Map of the City of Newport, 1937, Sampson & Murdock Co.,
Providence, R.I., 1937.

George Champlin Mason, Sr. *Newport and Its Cottages,*
Rand, Avery & Co., Boston, 1875.

*New York Times,* 28 June 1962, p. 33.

Van Rensselaer, Mary King. "Newport Our Social Capital,"
J. B. Lippincott Co., Philadelphia, 1905.

# CREDITS

## FRONT / BACK COVERS

**Front:** *Chetwode garden facade from the fountain basin, ca. 1935; The Preservation Society of Newport County.* **Back:** *Chetwode garden facade in ruin, 1973; The Preservation Society of Newport County.*

## INTRODUCTION

**Page 9:** *Ocean House Hotel (burned 1898), Briskham Jackson Photographer, ca. 1890; The Preservation Society of Newport County.* **Page 10:** *Bancroft Cottage, Rosecliff, Clarence Stanhope Photographer, ca. 1890; The Preservation Society of Newport County. Merritt Cottage, The Elms, later E.J. Berwind, Clarence Stanhope Photographer, ca. 1890; The Preservation Society of Newport County. Oakland Farm, entrance facade, Wurts Brothers Photographers, 1906; The Preservation Society of Newport County. Oakland Farm, garden facade, Wurts Brothers Photographers, 1906; The Preservation Society of Newport County.* **Page 11:** *Oakland Farm, riding ring, Wurts Brothers Photographers, 1906; The Preservation Society of Newport County.*

## THE COTTAGES

**Page 14:** *F.W. Andrews House, ca. 1895; courtesy of Shepley, Bulfinch, Richardson and Abbott.*
**Page 16:** *Castlewood drawing room. Photograph by Floyd E. Baker, 1919; The Preservation Society of Newport County.*
**Page 16:** *Castlewood, Alman & Co. Photographers, 1906; The Preservation Society of Newport County.*
**Page 17:** *Castlewood, Alman & Co. Photographers, ca. 1920; The Preservation Society of Newport County.*
**Page 18:** *Castlewood, Alman & Co. Photographers, 1906; The Preservation Society of Newport County.*
**Page 18:** *Castlewood, Alman & Co. Photographers, 1906; The Preservation Society of Newport County.*
**Page 18:** *Castlewood, Alman & Co. Photographers, 1906; The Preservation Society of Newport County.*
**Page 19:** *Residence of E.S. Philbrick, James R. Osgood & Co., 1876; The Preservation Society of Newport County.*
**Page 21:** *Bannister House, Meservey Photographer, 1947; The Preservation Society of Newport County.*
**Page 22:** *Dudley Place, ca. 1920; The Preservation Society of Newport County.*
**Page 26:** *Whitehall, ca. 1900; The Preservation Society of Newport County.*
**Page 26:** *Whitehall, ca. 1930; The Preservation Society of Newport County.*
**Page 27:** *Whitehall, ca. 1897; Clarence Stanhope Photographer; The Preservation Society of Newport County.*
**Page 29:** *The Corners, Ernst Studio Photography, ca. 1935; The Preservation Society of Newport County.*
**Page 30:** *T.G. Appleton House, ca. 1875; The Preservation Society of Newport County.*
**Page 32:** *Caldwell House, interior, ca. 1890; by courtesy of Historic New England.*
**Page 34:** *Gammell Cottage, ca. 1910; The Preservation Society of Newport County.*
**Page 36:** *H.A.C. Taylor Residence, Ticknor & Co., 1887; The Preservation Society of Newport County.*
**Page 37:** *H.A.C. Taylor House, Meservey Photographer, 1947; The Preservation Society of Newport County.*
**Page 38:** *H.A.C. Taylor House, ca. 1910; The Preservation Society of Newport County.*
**Page 38:** *H.A.C. Taylor House, Meservey Photographer, 1947; The Preservation Society of Newport County.*
**Page 39:** *Fearing Cottage, ca. 1875; The Preservation Society of Newport County.*
**Page 40:** *Croquet Party, ca. 1865; The Preservation Society of Newport County.*
**Page 41:** *Sheldon Cottage, ca. 1875; The Preservation Society of Newport County.*
**Page 42:** *Beach Cliffe, ca. 1875; The Preservation Society of Newport County.*
**Page 44:** *Linden Gate, Clarence Stanhope Photographer, ca. 1880; The Preservation Society of Newport County.*
**Page 44:** *Linden Gate, ca. 1897; The Preservation Society of Newport County.*
**Page 45:** *Linden Gate, Meservey Photographer, 1947; The Preservation Society of Newport County.*
**Page 46:** *Linden Gate, ca. 1883; The Preservation Society of Newport County.*
**Page 46:** *Linden Gate, 1951; The Preservation Society of Newport County.*

**Page 47:** *Pumpelly Cottage, ca. 1885; The Preservation Society of Newport County.*
**Page 47:** *Pumpelly Cottage, ca. 1890; The Preservation Society of Newport County.*
**Page 48:** *Ladd Villa, ca. 1897; The Preservation Society of Newport County.*
**Page 52:** *Stone Villa, ca. 1957; The Preservation Society of Newport County.*
**Page 52:** *Stone Villa, by M. Dobujinsky, 1949; The Preservation Society of Newport County.*
**Page 53:** *Stone Villa, ca. 1920; The Preservation Society of Newport County.*
**Page 54:** *Stone Villa, ca. 1955; The Preservation Society of Newport County.*
**Page 55:** *Paran Stevens Villa, ca. 1890; The Preservation Society of Newport County.*
**Page 56:** *Lady Paget as Cleopatra, 1897; The Preservation Society of Newport County.*
**Page 56:** *Paran Stevens Villa, ca. 1875; The Preservation Society of Newport County.*
**Page 57:** *Arleigh, ca. 1910; The Preservation Society of Newport County.*
**Page 58:** *Villa Rosa, Alman & Co. Photographers, 1904; The Preservation Society of Newport County.*
**Page 58:** *Villa Rosa, Alman & Co. Photographers, 1904; The Preservation Society of Newport County.*
**Page 59:** *Villa Rosa, Alman & Co. Photographers, 1904; The Preservation Society of Newport County.*
**Page 60:** *Villa Rosa, Alman & Co. Photographers, 1904; The Preservation Society of Newport County.*
**Page 61:** *Villa Rosa, Alman & Co. Photographers, 1904; The Preservation Society of Newport County.*
**Page 61:** *Villa Rosa, garden facade with the Haggin children. ca. 1915; private collection.*
**Page 62:** *Mrs. James B.A. Haggin, ca. 1915: The Preservation Society of Newport County.*
**Page 62:** *Villa Rosa, Ernst Studio Photography, ca. 1930; The Preservation Society of Newport County.*
**Page 63:** *G.H. Warren House, ca. 1920; The Preservation Society of Newport County.*
**Page 64:** *Whitney Warren House, ca. 1920; The Preservation Society of Newport County.*
**Page 65:** *Whiteholme, Alman & Co. Photographers, ca. 1905; The Preservation Society of Newport County.*
**Page 64:** *Whiteholme, J. Rugen Photographer, ca. 1930; The Preservation Society of Newport County.*
**Page 65:** *Whiteholme, Alman & Co. Photographers, ca. 1905; The Preservation Society of Newport County.*
**Page 66:** *Whiteholme, Alman & Co. Photographers, ca. 1905; The Preservation Society of Newport County.*
**Page 67:** *Whiteholme, ca. 1945; The Preservation Society of Newport County.*
**Page 68:** *Whiteholme, Alman & Co. Photographers, ca. 1905; The Preservation Society of Newport County.*
**Page 69:** *Sulthorne, ca. 1970; The Preservation Society of Newport County.*
**Page 69:** *Sulthorne, 1973; The Preservation Society of Newport County.*
**Page 70:** *Greystone, Clarence Stanhope Photographer, ca. 1890; The Preservation Society of Newport County.*
**Page 70:** *Greystone, ca. 1890; The Preservation Society of Newport County.*
**Page 71:** *Greystone, ca. 1890; The Preservation Society of Newport County.*
**Page 72:** *The Cloister, Town End Studio Photographer, ca. 1930; by courtesy of The Newport Historical Society.*
**Page 72:** *The Cloister, Town End Studio Photographer, ca. 1930; by courtesy of The Newport Historical Society.*
**Page 73:** *The Cloister, ca. 1930; The Preservation Society of Newport County.*
**Page 74:** *D'Hauteville Cottage, ca. 1875; The Preservation Society of Newport County.*
**Page 76:** *Stoneacre, ca. 1888; The Preservation Society of Newport County.*
**Page 77:** *Stoneacre, Ernst Studio Photographers, ca. 1930; The Preservation Society of Newport County.*
**Page 78:** *Chetwode, Ernst Studio Photographers, ca. 1935; The Preservation Society of Newport County.*
**Page 78:** *Chetwode, Architectural Review Vol 11, No. 6, plate 34; The Preservation Society of Newport County.*
**Page 79:** *Chetwode, ca. 1910; The Preservation Society of Newport County.*
**Page 80:** *Chetwode, ca. 1910; The Preservation Society of Newport County.*
**Page 81:** *Chetwode, ca. 1930; The Preservation Society of Newport County.*

Page 81:     Chetwode, ca. 1930; The Preservation Society of Newport County.
Page 82:     Chetwode, ca. 1930; The Preservation Society of Newport County.
Page 82:     Chetwode, ca. 1930; The Preservation Society of Newport County.
Page 83:     Chetwode, ca. 1930; The Preservation Society of Newport County.
Page 83:     Chetwode, ca. 1930; The Preservation Society of Newport County.
Page 84:     Mrs. August Belmont, oil on canvas portrait, ca. 1870; The Preservation Society
             of Newport County.
Page 84:     Mrs. Belmont in carriage, ca. 1870; The Preservation Society of Newport County.
Page 85:     By-the-Sea, ca. 1875; The Preservation Society of Newport County.
Page 86:     By-the-Sea, ca. 1930; The Preservation Society of Newport County.
Page 86:     By-the-Sea, ca. 1910; The Preservation Society of Newport County.
Page 87:     W.W. Tucker House, ca. 1875; The Preservation Society of Newport County.
Page 89:     Hawthorne Villa, ca. 1910; The Preservation Society of Newport County.
Page 90:     The Reefs, ca. 1875; The Preservation Society of Newport County.
Page 90:     The Reefs, Frank Child Photographer, ca. 1898; The Preservation Society of Newport County.
Page 91:     The Reefs, from an engraving by John Collins, 1857; The Preservation Society of
             Newport County.
Page 92:     The Reefs, ca. 1930; The Preservation Society of Newport County.
Page 92:     The Reefs, ca. 1935; The Preservation Society of Newport County.
Page 93:     Reef Point, ca. 1890; The Preservation Society of Newport County.
Page 95:     Gull Rock, Thomas Zinn Photographer, ca. 1955; The Preservation Society of Newport County.
Page 96:     Seaverge, Ernst Studio Photographers, ca. 1930; The Preservation Society of
             Newport County.
Page 96:     Seaverge, ca.1955; by courtesy of Mrs. Harle Tinney.
Page 96:     Seaverge, ca.1955; by courtesy of Mrs. Harle Tinney.
Page 97:     Seaverge, ca.1955; by courtesy of Mrs. Harle Tinney.
Page 98:     Rockhurst, T.E. Geisler Photographer, ca. 1923; The Preservation Society of Newport
             County.
Page 99:     Rockhurst, Clarence Stanhope Photographer, ca. 1898; The Preservation Society of
             Newport County.
Page 100:    Mrs. Walter B. James, Donald P. Thurston Photographer, ca. 1940; The Preservation Society
             of Newport County.
Page 100:    Rockhurst, Aspegren Ball, J. Rugen Photographer, 1923; The Preservation Society of
             Newport County.
Page 100:    Rockhurst, J. Rugen Photographer, 1923; The Preservation Society of Newport County.
Page 101:    Beachholm, ca. 1890; The Preservation Society of Newport County.
Page 102:    Beachholm, ca. 1920; The Preservation Society of Newport County.
Page 102:    Beachholm, Meservey Photographer, 1947; The Preservation Society of Newport County.
Page 103:    R. Baker House, ca. 1925; by courtesy of Ms. Theodora Aspegren.
Page 104:    R. Baker House, H.O. Havemeyer Photographer, 1919; The Preservation Society
             of Newport County.
Page 105:    Cadwalader House, ca. 1925; The Preservation Society of Newport County.
Page 108:    The Rocks, Clarence Stanhope Photographer, ca. 1890; The Preservation Society of Newport
             County.
Page 108:    The Rocks, ca. 1930; The Preservation Society of Newport County.
Page 108:    The Rocks, ca. 1920; The Preservation Society of Newport County.
Page 109:    The Rocks, H.O. Havemeyer Photographer, 1938; The Preservation Society of
             Newport County.
Page 110:    Seafield, ca. 1950; The Preservation Society of Newport County.
Page 112:    Beacon Hill House, ca. 1937; The Preservation Society of Newport County.
Page 112:    Beacon Hill House, ca. 1947; The Preservation Society of Newport County.
Page 112:    Beacon Hill House, Alman & Co. Photographers, ca. 1912;
             The Preservation Society of Newport County.
Page 113:    Beacon Hill House, Alman & Co. Photographers, ca. 1912;
             The Preservation Society of Newport County.
Page 114:    Beacon Hill House, Ernst Studio Photographers, ca. 1920; The Preservation Society of
             Newport County.

**Page 115:** *Beacon Hill House, Alman & Co. Photographers, ca. 1912; The Preservation Society of Newport County.*

**Page 115:** *Beacon Hill House, Alman & Co. Photographers, ca. 1912; The Preservation Society of Newport County.*

**Page 115:** *Beacon Hill House, Alman & Co. Photographers, ca. 1912; The Preservation Society of Newport County.*

**Page 116:** *The Reef, Clarence Stanhope Photographer, ca. 1890; The Preservation Society of Newport County.*

**Page 116:** *The Reef, Mrs. John C. Fairchild Photographer, ca. 1914; The Preservation Society of Newport County.*

**Page 116:** *The Reef, ca. 1920; The Preservation Society of Newport County.*

**Page 117:** *The Reef, ca. 1920; The Preservation Society of Newport County.*

**Page 118:** *The Reef, ca. 1920; The Preservation Society of Newport County.*

**Page 118:** *The Reef, 1928; by courtesy of The Newport Historical Society.*

**Page 119:** *Bleak House, ca. 1897; The Preservation Society of Newport County.*

**Page 120:** *Bleak House, ca. 1920; The Preservation Society of Newport County.*

**Page 121:** *Bateman's, Ernst Studio Photographers, ca. 1930; The Preservation Society of Newport County.*

**Page 122:** *Bateman's Hotel, Ernst Studio Photographers, ca. 1930; The Preservation Society of Newport County.*

**Page 123:** *Sunset Ridge, from an engraving in Richard M. Bayles,* History of Newport County, *1888; by courtesy of The Redwood Library and Athenaeum.*

**Page 124:** *Armsea Hall, Mrs. John C. Fairchild Photographer, ca. 1914; The Preservation Society of Newport County.*

**Page 124:** *Armsea Hall, Mrs. John C. Fairchild Photographer, ca. 1914; The Preservation Society of Newport County.*

**Page 124:** *Armsea Hall, Thomas Zinn Photographer, 1955; The Preservation Society of Newport County.*

**Page 125:** *Armsea Hall, ca. 1940; The Preservation Society of Newport County.*

**Page 126:** *Armsea Hall, Mrs. John C. Fairchild Photographer, ca. 1914; The Preservation Society of Newport County.*

**Page 127:** *Vedimar, ca. 1930; The Preservation Society of Newport County.*

**Page 128:** *Vedimar, 1974; The Preservation Society of Newport County.*

**Page 128:** *Vedimar, 1974; The Preservation Society of Newport County.*

**Page 129:** *Pen Craig, Town End Studio Photographers, ca. 1930; by courtesy of The Newport Historical Society.*

**Page 130:** *Harbourview, ca. 1897; The Preservation Society of Newport County.*

**Page 131:** *Harbourview, ca. 1910; The Preservation Society of Newport County.*

# INDEX TO THE COTTAGES

Andrews, F.W., House (Sunset Lawn); p. 15

Appleton, T.G., House; p. 31

Arleigh; p. 57

Armsea Hall; p. 125

Baker, R. Jr. House, (Westcliff); p. 103

Bannister, J., House; p. 21

Bateman's; p. 121

Beach Cliffe; p. 43

Beachholm (Train Villa); p. 101

Beacon Hill House; p. 113

Bleak House; p. 119

By-the-Sea; p. 85

Cadwalader Cottage; p. 105

Caldwell House; p. 33

Castlewood; p. 17

Chetwode; p. 79

Cloister, The; p. 73

Corners, The; p. 29

Dudley, C., House (Dudley Place); p. 23

Fearing, D., Cottage; p. 39

Gammell, W. Cottage; p. 35

Greystone; p. 71

Gull Rock; p. 95

Harbourview; p. 131

D'Hauteville, F.S.G., Cottage; p. 75

Hawthorne Villa; p. 89

Ladd Villa; p. 49

Linden Gate; p. 45

Pen Craig; p. 129

Philbrick, E., Cottage; p. 19

Pumpelly Cottage; p. 47

Reef, The; p. 117

Reef Point; p. 93

Reefs, The (Whitney Cottage); p. 91

Rockhurst; p. 99

Rocks, The; p. 109

Seafield; p. 111

Seaverge; p. 97

Sheldon, F., House; p. 41

Stevens, P., Villa; p. 55

Stone Villa; p. 53

Stoneacre; p. 77

Sulthorne; p. 69

Sunset Lawn (F.W. Andrews House); p. 15

Sunset Ridge; p. 123

Taylor, H.A.C., House; p. 37

Train Villa (Beachholm); p. 101

Tucker, W.W., House; p. 87

Vedimar; p. 127

Villa Rosa; p. 59

Warren, G.H., House; p. 63

Warren, W., House; p. 64

Westcliff (R. Baker Jr. house); p. 103

Whitehall; p. 27

Whiteholme; p. 67

Whitney Cottage (The Reefs); p. 91

LaVergne, TN USA
20 December 2010
209610LV00001B